Repentance Revealed The Road Back To God

Joshua Rhoades

Published by Joshua Paul Rhoades, 2024.

REPENTANCE REVEALED THE ROAD BACK TO GOD

First edition. October 9, 2024.

Copyright © 2024 Joshua Rhoades.

ISBN: 979-8227108265

Written by Joshua Rhoades.

Also by Joshua Rhoades

Courage Under Fire: David's Stand On The Battlefield
Jonah's Journey: Voices Of Redemption And Lessons In Obedience
The Furnace Of Faith: 12 Principles From The Heat Of Faith
Whispers of Hope: Inspiring Stories of Men's Prayers In Scripture
Frontier Legends: The Oregon Dream
Elijah: A Beacon Of Boldness
HOOK, LINE & SAVIOUR - Faith Reflections from Fishing
Driven By Faith: Motor Racing Inspired Christian Life
30 Day Devotional - Bold and Strong- Coffee Devotions for a Courageous
Christian Walk
Authentic Christianity: The Heart of Old Time Religion
Consider The Ant - God's Tiny Preachers
Flee Fornication: The Plea For Purity
Renewed Hope- How to Find Encouragement in God
Sounding The Call - The Voice of Conviction
The Altar - Where Heaven Meets Earth
The Bible's Battlefields- Timeless Lessons from Ancient Wars
The Sacred Art of Silence - How Silence Speaks in Scripture
Under Fire- The Sanctity of the Traditional Biblical Home
Who Is on the Lord's Side? A Call to Righteousness
What Is Truth? - From Skepticism to Submission
First and Goal- Faith and Football Fundamentals
From Dugout to Devotion- Spiritual Lessons from Baseball
Par for the Course- Faith and Fairways
The Believer's Pace- Tools for Running Life's Marathon
The Immutable Fortress- Security in God's Unchanging Nature
Biblical Bravery
Deer Stands and Devotions: A Hunter's Walk with God

Jesus Knows- Our Hearts, Our Responsibility

Restoration - Setting The Bone

Spiritual 911- God's Word for Life's Emergency's

The Freedom of Forgiveness

The Jezebel Effect - Ancient Manipulations Modern Lessons

The Shout That Stopped The Saviour

The Time Machine Chronicles: Old Testament Characters

Anchored In Truth Exploring The Depths of Psalm 119

Biblical Counsel on Anger

Proverbs' Portraits The Men God Mentions

Stumbling in the Dark - The Dangers of Alcohol

Guarding the Wicket Protecting Your Faith and Game

The Champion's Faith - Wrestling and Achieving Spiritual Victory

Scriptural Commands for Modern Times Living God's Word Today Volume 1

Scriptural Commands for Modern Times Living God's Word Today Volume 2

Scriptural Commands for Modern Times Living God's Word TodayVolume3

The Greatest Gift

A Christmas Journey of Faith

Daughter Of The King: Embracing Your Identity In Christ

Determination and Dedication Building Strong Faith As A Young Man

Walking Through Walls God's Power to Part the Storms of Life

David's Song Of Deliverance Praising God Through Every Storm

From Weakness to Warrior: Gideon's Transformation

Why Did Jesus Weep?

Living For God The Call To Be A Living Sacrifice

My Mind Is In A Fog What Do I Do?

Turning The Page Written By Grace

The Calling and Greatness of John the Baptist

For Such a Time Esther's Courageous Stand

From Brokenness To Beauty Written By The Pen of Grace

The Ultimate Guide to Massive Action- From Plans to Reality

A Heart Of Conviction

Serving In The Shadows

Repentance Revealed The Road Back To God

The Chief Sinner Meets The Chief Saviour Reflections On I Timothy 1:15

Dedication

To You, the Reader,

This book is for you—the one seeking more. The one who may feel the weight of life pressing down, wondering if there is a way back to peace, hope, and purpose. Whether you're carrying the guilt of past mistakes, the burden of regret, or simply the deep longing to be closer to God, "Repentance Revealed – The Road Back to God" is dedicated to your journey. It is for the times you've felt distant from Him, for the moments when you've questioned if it's too late to return, and for the quiet, unspoken prayers of your heart asking, "Can I still be forgiven?"

You are not alone. Every one of us has wandered, every one of us has struggled with the weight of our own choices, the shadows of our past, and the fear that we've drifted too far from God's grace. But this book exists to tell you something crucial: there is a way back. The road to God is not closed, no matter how far you've gone or how long you've been away. This road is one of repentance, and it leads straight to the heart of a God who loves you more deeply than you can imagine.

Repentance is not a word to be feared. It's not about shame or punishment—it's about restoration. It's about healing. It's about turning away from what has harmed you and returning to the One who can heal and renew your soul. I want you to know that repentance is not a single moment in time; it's a journey. A road that you can walk every day, step by step, as you grow closer to God and experience the freedom He offers.

This book is dedicated to your freedom. It is dedicated to your healing. It is dedicated to showing you that no matter where you've been, God is waiting for you with open arms. Repentance is the key that unlocks the door to the fullness of life He has prepared for you—a life free from guilt, shame, and the burdens that weigh you down. It is an invitation to let go of the chains that have held you back and to walk forward in the light of His grace.

My hope is that as you read this book, you will feel the powerful truth that repentance is not a sign of weakness, but of strength. It is the road of courage, where you choose to confront the things that have held you captive and declare that they will no longer have power over you. It is the road of hope, where you trust that God's grace is greater than your past. It is the road of love, where you experience the depths of God's forgiveness and realize that He has never stopped loving you—not for a moment.

This book is your guide back to the heart of God. As you walk this road of repentance, may you find peace in knowing that God is with you every step of the way. May you experience the joy of being forgiven, the relief of laying down your burdens, and the freedom of living in God's grace. "Repentance Revealed – The Road Back to God" is dedicated to you, to your journey, and to the beautiful truth that the way back to God is always open. You are loved, you are forgiven, and you are never too far from His embrace.

Introduction

Life is full of moments when we feel lost, burdened, or disconnected. We may find ourselves drifting from the sense of peace and purpose that once anchored our lives. Whether it's due to poor decisions, the weight of guilt, or simply the pressures of life, we all have times when we feel far from God. The good news is that no matter how far we've wandered, the road back to God is always open. This road, so beautifully laid out in Scripture, is the path of repentance—a journey that leads us away from sin, into God's loving arms, and back to the fullness of life that He desires for us.

"Repentance Revealed: The Road Back to God" is about discovering and embracing this sacred journey. Repentance is not a word that should stir fear or shame. Instead, it is an invitation to start fresh, to release the burdens of sin, and to experience the incredible grace of God. Throughout the Bible, from the Old Testament to the New Testament, repentance is a key theme. Time and again, God calls His people to turn back to Him, offering mercy and forgiveness. Whether it's through the messages of the prophets, the teachings of Jesus, or the writings of the apostles, the call to repentance is one of love and restoration.

For many, the concept of repentance may seem difficult or even overwhelming. It can feel like an acknowledgment of failure or a reminder of guilt. But repentance is not about dwelling on the past or wallowing in regret. Instead, it is a life-giving process that restores us to God's original design and purpose for our lives. It is the key that unlocks the door to spiritual freedom, healing, and transformation. When we repent, we are not just turning away from sin; we are turning toward something much greater—God's boundless grace, His perfect love, and the abundant life He promises.

The journey of repentance begins with a decision—a decision to acknowledge our need for God and to turn away from anything that separates us from Him. This is not about perfection or earning God's love; it's about humbly recognizing that we can't do life on our own, and that we need His guidance and grace. Repentance requires honesty with ourselves and with God, but it also brings with it a deep sense of relief. When we confess our sins, God is faithful and just to forgive us (1 John 1:9). There is nothing more freeing than knowing that we can leave our mistakes, shame, and guilt behind and walk forward in newness of life.

This book will walk you through the steps of repentance as revealed in the Bible, showing how this sacred process is not about punishment but about restoration. Each chapter will explore a different aspect of repentance—how it brings freedom from sin, delivers us from guilt, and opens the door to a closer relationship with God. We will look at the stories of individuals in Scripture who experienced deep transformation through repentance: people like King David, who after falling into sin, cried out for a clean heart and found God's mercy; the people of Nineveh, who repented at Jonah's warning and were spared from destruction; and the apostle Peter, who after denying Jesus, wept bitterly and was restored by the Lord's love.

Repentance is not just a one-time event but an ongoing posture of the heart. It is something we must continually embrace as we walk with God. Life is full of challenges, temptations, and moments when we fall short. But through repentance, we can continually realign our hearts with God's will, seeking His forgiveness and direction for our lives. This book will show you that repentance is not about focusing on our failures, but about experiencing God's faithfulness. It's about trusting that no matter how many times we stumble, God is always ready to lift us up when we turn back to Him.

In a world that often glorifies self-reliance and independence, repentance reminds us of our dependence on God. It teaches us that true strength is found in humility, and that healing begins when we admit our need for God's help. As you read this book, my hope is that you will be encouraged to embrace repentance not as something to fear but as a beautiful, life-giving journey back to God. You will see that repentance is not just about acknowledging where we've gone wrong, but about receiving God's grace and stepping into the fullness of His plan for your life.

The road of repentance is one we all must walk, but it is not a road we walk alone. God walks with us every step of the way, guiding us, comforting us, and celebrating our return to Him. "Repentance Revealed – The Road Back To

God" will show you that no matter how far you've strayed or how heavy the burdens of life may feel, God is always calling you back to Himself with open arms. The road back to God is paved with grace, and repentance is the key that unlocks the door to the life He has prepared for you.

As you take this journey through the pages of this book, I invite you to open your heart to God's transforming love. Let go of the fear, guilt, or shame that may have held you back. Repentance is not a punishment—it's an opportunity to be renewed, restored, and set free. The road back to God is waiting for you, and it's a road that leads to joy, peace, and the abundant life that only He can provide. May this book be a source of hope and encouragement as you walk the path of repentance and discover the beauty of returning to the heart of God.

Chapter 1 – Decision

Repentance, according to the Bible, always begins with a conscious decision to turn from sin and turn toward God. This decision is not just a fleeting thought or a passing feeling but a purposeful and deliberate choice. It's a decision that involves both the mind and the heart, recognizing the wrongness of sin and the need to return to God. This choice is seen clearly in the story of the Prodigal Son, which is found in Luke 15:18-20. The Prodigal Son, after wasting his inheritance and finding himself in a desperate situation, finally comes to his senses and says, "I will arise and go to my father, and will say unto him, Father, I have sinned against heaven, and before thee, And am no more worthy to be called thy son: make me as one of thy hired servants. And he arose, and came to his father." This moment of decision is the turning point in his life. He made a conscious choice to leave his life of sin behind and return to his father, symbolizing repentance and restoration. The Prodigal Son's decision was not an easy one, as it required humility, honesty, and a willingness to admit his mistakes. But it was this decision that led him back into the loving arms of his father, just as repentance brings us back into the grace and forgiveness of God.

In the same way, John the Baptist preached repentance, urging people to make a life-changing decision to turn from their sins. In Matthew 3:1-2, it says, "In those days came John the Baptist, preaching in the wilderness of Judaea, And saying, Repent ye: for the kingdom of heaven is at hand." John's message was clear: repentance begins with a decision, a decision to turn away from sinful behaviors and attitudes and to turn toward God and His ways. He called the people to make a deliberate choice to leave their old lives behind and to prepare their hearts for the coming of the Lord. John's preaching was powerful, and it caused many to reflect on their lives and make the decision to change. He was not asking people to make a temporary adjustment or a small improvement in their behavior—he was calling for a radical and complete turning of the heart and mind, a decision that would change the course of their lives forever.

The decision to repent is the first and most important step in the process of coming back to God. It is a moment of realization when a person acknowledges their sinfulness, feels the weight of their wrongdoing, and decides that they no longer want to live in separation from God. The decision to repent is an act of the will, a conscious choice to reject sin and to seek God's forgiveness. This decision is often accompanied by a deep sense of sorrow for the ways in which a person has offended God and hurt others. In 2 Corinthians 7:10, Paul writes, "For godly sorrow worketh repentance to salvation not to be repented of: but the sorrow of the world worketh death." True repentance begins with this godly sorrow, a sorrow that leads to a genuine decision to change and seek God's mercy.

However, making the decision to repent is not always easy. It requires a person to confront their sin, to be honest with themselves about their need for change, and to be willing to surrender their pride. The Prodigal Son had to swallow his pride and admit that he had made a mess of his life. He had to acknowledge that he had sinned not only against his earthly father but also against God. Similarly, anyone who makes the decision to repent must come to terms with their own sinfulness and their need for God's forgiveness. It's a humbling process, but it's also the first step toward healing and restoration.

One of the reasons why repentance requires a decision is because sin often has a strong grip on a person's life. Sin is deceptive, and it can make a person feel trapped, as if there is no way out. But repentance offers a way of escape, a path that leads back to God. In Romans 6:23, it says, "For the wages of sin is death; but the gift of God is eternal life through Jesus Christ our Lord." Sin leads to death, both spiritually and sometimes physically, but repentance opens the door to life. It's a choice between continuing down a path that leads to destruction or turning around and heading toward life in Christ. That's why repentance is a decision—it's a turning point, a moment when a person decides to change the direction of their life and follow God instead of following their sinful desires.

The decision to repent is not something that should be delayed or put off until a later time. In Hebrews 3:15, it says, "To day if ye will hear his voice, harden not your hearts." God calls people to make the decision to repent today, not tomorrow or sometime in the future. There's a sense of urgency in the Bible's message about repentance because none of us knows how much time we have. Life is fragile, and the opportunity to turn to God is something that should be seized immediately. Just as John the Baptist called people to repent because "the kingdom of heaven is at hand," we too are living in a time when we need to make the decision to repent without delay. The consequences of delaying repentance are serious, as continued sin hardens the heart and makes it more difficult to turn back to God.

But when a person does make the decision to repent, there is great joy and celebration in heaven. In Luke 15:7, Jesus says, "I say unto you, that likewise joy shall be in heaven over one sinner that repenteth, more than over ninety and nine just persons, which need no repentance." The decision to repent is not just a personal victory—it's a cause for rejoicing in heaven. God delights in seeing His children turn back to Him, and He is ready to welcome them with open arms, just as the father welcomed the Prodigal Son. When we make the decision to repent, we are not met with condemnation or judgment—we are met with grace, mercy, and forgiveness.

Repentance is also a decision that leads to action. It's not enough to simply decide to change; true repentance is followed by a change in behavior. In Matthew 3:8, John the Baptist says, "Bring forth therefore fruits meet for repentance." This means that repentance should be evident in the way a person lives their life. The decision to turn from sin and turn toward God must be accompanied by actions that reflect that change. For the Prodigal Son, this meant not just deciding to return to his father but actually getting up and making the journey home. Similarly, when we make the decision to repent, we must follow through by turning away from sinful behaviors and actively seeking to live in obedience to God.

The decision to repent is also a decision to accept God's grace. Repentance is not about trying to earn God's forgiveness through good works or by being perfect—it's about turning to God in faith and trusting in His mercy. Ephesians 2:8-9 says, "For by grace are ye saved through faith; and that not of yourselves: it is the gift of God: Not of works, lest any man should boast." Repentance is about recognizing that we cannot save ourselves, that we are completely dependent on God's grace for our salvation. The decision to repent is a decision to trust in the finished work of Jesus Christ on the cross, to believe that His sacrifice is sufficient to cover all of our sins, and to receive the gift of forgiveness that He offers.

In conclusion, repentance begins with a decision—a decision to turn from sin and turn toward God. This decision is a crucial first step in the process of coming back to God and experiencing His forgiveness and grace. The story of the Prodigal Son shows us that no matter how far we've wandered, we can always make the decision to return to the Father. John the Baptist's preaching reminds us that repentance is urgent and necessary, and it requires a deliberate choice to change the direction of our lives. The decision to repent is not easy, but it is the key to finding freedom from sin and entering into a restored relationship with God. It's a decision that leads to joy, both in our own hearts and in heaven, and it's a decision that can change the course of our lives forever. When we decide to repent, we are choosing to step onto the road back to God, and He is always ready to welcome us with open arms.

Chapter 2 - Desire for Change

True repentance begins with a deep, genuine desire for change, a longing that moves the heart to turn away from sin and to seek a transformed life in God. This desire is not just a temporary feeling of guilt or shame but a sincere yearning for a new beginning and a clean heart. This is beautifully reflected in the plea of David in Psalm 51:10, where he cries out, "Create in me a clean heart, O God; and renew a right spirit within me." David, having committed grievous sins, was broken by the weight of his guilt and sought not just forgiveness but an inner transformation—a clean heart and a renewed spirit. His prayer was more than a request to be forgiven; it was an appeal to be changed from the inside out, to have his very nature cleansed and restored to align with God's holiness. This desire for change is the heartbeat of true repentance, the kind of repentance that moves beyond mere regret for wrongdoing and seeks a new way of living that is pleasing to God. David's plea echoes the cry of every repentant heart, a cry that longs not only for the removal of guilt but for the creation of something new, something pure, something that reflects God's righteousness.

Jesus echoed this call for change when He began His ministry, urging people to repent and change their ways. In Matthew 4:17, it says, "From that time Jesus began to preach, and to say, Repent: for the kingdom of heaven is at hand." Jesus was calling people to do more than just acknowledge their sins; He was calling them to a radical transformation of their lives, to turn from sin and embrace a new life in the kingdom of God. His message was clear: repentance is not simply about feeling sorry for what we've done wrong, but about desiring and pursuing a new direction, a new way of living that reflects God's will. This desire for change is central to repentance because without it, there can be no true turning away from sin. It is the driving force that leads a person to seek God's forgiveness and to commit to living according to His commandments.

Jesus' call to repentance is a call to change not only outward actions but the inward condition of the heart, just as David longed for in his prayer for a clean heart.

The desire for change in true repentance is also marked by a recognition that we cannot change ourselves by our own strength. David's prayer in Psalm 51 is a humble acknowledgment of his inability to cleanse his own heart. He turns to God, asking, "Create in me a clean heart," because he knows that only God has the power to transform his sinful heart into something pure and righteous. This teaches us that the desire for change in repentance must be accompanied by a reliance on God's grace and power. We cannot achieve true change through our own efforts or willpower alone. We must turn to God, acknowledging our weakness and asking Him to do the work of transformation within us. True repentance, then, is not just a desire to stop sinning; it is a desire for God to reshape our hearts, to remove the sinful desires that have taken root, and to replace them with a heart that seeks after Him.

This desire for change also involves a deep sense of dissatisfaction with sin. When a person truly repents, they no longer find satisfaction in the things that once brought them pleasure. Instead, they begin to see sin for what it truly is—destructive, harmful, and a barrier to a relationship with God. This was the case with David, who, after being confronted with his sin, was deeply grieved by what he had done. His desire for a clean heart came from a place of recognizing the damage his sin had caused, both to himself and to others, and most importantly, the offense it had caused against God. True repentance involves this same recognition: that sin is not something to be taken lightly or excused, but something that separates us from the God who loves us. It is this recognition that fuels the desire for change, the longing to turn away from sin and to live a life that honors God.

The desire for change in repentance also brings about a renewed sense of purpose. When a person repents, they are not only seeking to be forgiven for past mistakes, but they are also seeking to live differently in the future. This is why David's prayer in Psalm 51 includes the request for a "right spirit" to be renewed within him. He wanted more than just forgiveness; he wanted the strength and determination to live a life that was aligned with God's will. True repentance involves a commitment to live differently, to pursue righteousness and to seek God's guidance in every area of life. This is why Jesus, when calling people to repent, was inviting them into a new way of life—life in the kingdom of God, where their actions, thoughts, and desires would be transformed by the power of God's grace.

The desire for change in true repentance also involves a willingness to let go of the past. Often, people hold onto guilt, shame, or the patterns of sin that have defined their lives for so long. But true repentance means letting go of those things and allowing God to make all things new. In 2 Corinthians 5:17, Paul writes, "Therefore if any man be in Christ, he is a new creature: old things are passed away; behold, all things are become new." This is the promise of repentance—that through God's grace, we can leave the old life behind and walk in the newness of life that He offers. But this requires a desire for change, a willingness to release the past and to embrace the future that God has for us. Just as David sought a clean heart and a renewed spirit, so too must we seek to let go of our old ways and allow God to create something new in us.

True repentance, motivated by a desire for change, also leads to a deeper relationship with God. When we repent and turn from our sins, we draw closer to God, and He draws closer to us. James 4:8 says, "Draw nigh to God, and he will draw nigh to you. Cleanse your hands, ye sinners; and purify your hearts, ye double minded." This is the essence of repentance—a drawing near to God, a cleansing of our hearts, and a desire to live in closer fellowship with Him. Repentance is not just about turning away from sin; it is about turning toward God and seeking to grow in our relationship with Him. The desire for change in repentance is ultimately a desire to know God more fully, to experience His presence in our lives, and to live in the freedom and joy that comes from walking in obedience to His will.

The desire for change in repentance also leads to lasting transformation. Repentance is not a temporary change or a momentary decision; it is a lifelong process of being transformed into the image of Christ. Romans 12:2 says, "And be not conformed to this world: but be ye transformed by the renewing of your mind, that ye may prove what is that good, and acceptable, and perfect, will of God." This transformation begins with a desire for change, a desire to no longer conform to the patterns of the world but to be renewed and shaped by God's Word and His Spirit. True repentance leads to lasting change because it is motivated by a deep desire to become more like Christ, to live in a way that reflects His love, His holiness, and His grace.

Finally, the desire for change in repentance is a gift from God. It is not something that we can muster up on our own; it is something that God works in our hearts by His grace. In Philippians 2:13, it says, "For it is God which worketh in you both to will and to do of his good pleasure." The very desire to repent, to turn from sin and to seek a new life in God, is a work of His Spirit within us. This means that repentance is not something we accomplish by our own efforts; it is a response to God's call and His grace at work in our lives. Just as David cried out for God to create in him a clean heart, so too must we rely on God's grace to transform us and give us the desire for change that leads to true repentance.

In conclusion, true repentance is motivated by a deep and genuine desire for change—a desire to turn away from sin and to live a life that is pleasing to God. This desire is beautifully expressed in David's plea in Psalm 51:10, "Create in me a clean heart, O God," a prayer that reflects his longing for transformation and renewal. Jesus' call to repentance in Matthew 4:17 reminds us that repentance is not just about feeling sorry for our sins; it is about a radical change of heart and life, a turning away from sin and a turning toward God. This desire for change is the foundation of true repentance, and it is a desire that leads to lasting transformation, a deeper relationship with God, and a life that reflects His love and holiness. Repentance is not something we can do on our own; it is a response to God's grace and a work of His Spirit within us. When we repent with a true desire for change, we open our hearts to God's transforming power, and we begin a journey of renewal and restoration that leads to the fullness of life that He has promised.

Chapter 3 – Determination

Repentance is more than just feeling sorrow for past sins; it is a deep commitment to change, and that commitment requires strong determination. When a person repents, they make a decision to turn away from sin and turn toward God, but making that decision is only the beginning. To truly repent, a person must have the determination to follow through on that commitment to change. Repentance involves not just a change of heart, but a change of behavior, a turning away from sinful actions and a deliberate effort to live according to God's commandments. This is clearly emphasized in Acts 26:20, where Paul speaks about his ministry and how he declared "first unto them of Damascus, and at Jerusalem, and throughout all the coasts of Judaea, and then to the Gentiles, that they should repent and turn to God, and do works meet for repentance." In this verse, Paul explains that repentance is not merely a matter of saying the right words or feeling regret; it must be proven through actions—through a life that reflects a genuine turning away from sin and a commitment to follow God. This requires strong determination, because the process of changing one's ways and living in obedience to God's Word is not always easy. It takes effort, perseverance, and a willingness to resist the temptations that once held power over us.

Determination is a crucial aspect of repentance because without it, a person's resolve to change may quickly fade. When Peter stood before the crowd on the day of Pentecost and preached to them about the need for repentance, he was calling them not just to feel remorse for their sins, but to make a firm decision to change their lives. In Acts 2:38, Peter says, "Repent, and be baptized every one of you in the name of Jesus Christ for the remission of sins, and ye shall receive the gift of the Holy Ghost." Repentance, as Peter described it, was the starting point for a new life in Christ, a life that would require determination and commitment. The act of being baptized was an outward sign of an inward change, a public declaration that the person had repented and was now determined to live a new life in Christ. But baptism was just the beginning—living out that new life would require daily determination to follow God's ways and to resist the pull of sin.

The need for determination in repentance is evident throughout the Bible. Time and again, we see examples of people who repented but needed strong determination to stay on the right path. One such example is found in the life of Zacchaeus, the tax collector who repented after meeting Jesus. In Luke 19:8, Zacchaeus stands before the Lord and says, "Behold, Lord, the half of my goods I give to the poor; and if I have taken any thing from any man by false accusation, I restore him fourfold." Zacchaeus didn't just say he was sorry for his wrongdoings—he was determined to make things right. His repentance was proven by his actions, as he made a deliberate effort to correct the wrongs he had done. This is the kind of determination that true repentance requires. It is not enough to feel guilty or ashamed of past sins; repentance means taking steps to change, to make amends where possible, and to live in a way that honors God.

Determination is also necessary because repentance often involves breaking free from deeply ingrained habits or behaviors. Sin can be addictive, and the patterns of sin can be hard to break. That's why repentance requires more than just good intentions—it requires a firm, unshakable determination to change. In Romans 12:2, Paul writes, "And be not conformed to this world: but be ye transformed by the renewing of your mind, that ye may prove what is that good, and acceptable, and perfect, will of God." This transformation of the mind is a key part of repentance, but it doesn't happen overnight. It requires determination to continually renew one's mind through prayer, studying the Bible, and seeking God's guidance. The world is constantly trying to pull people back into old ways of thinking and living, but a person who has truly repented must be determined to resist that pull and to stay focused on God's will.

The process of repentance can also be challenging because it often involves facing opposition or criticism from others. When a person decides to turn away from sin and live a life of righteousness, not everyone around them will be supportive. Some may mock or criticize their decision, while others may try to tempt them back into sinful behaviors. This is why determination is so important—without it, a person may be swayed by the opinions or actions of others and give up on their commitment to change. Jesus spoke about this in Matthew 7:13-14, where He says, "Enter ye in at the strait gate: for wide is the gate, and broad is the way, that leadeth to destruction, and many there be which go in thereat: Because strait is the gate, and narrow is the way, which leadeth unto life, and few there be that find it." The narrow way that leads to life is not an easy path, and walking it requires determination. Repentance is the decision to enter that narrow gate, but determination is what keeps a person walking the path, even when it's difficult or lonely.

The strength of determination in repentance is often tested over time. It's one thing to make a decision to repent in a moment of conviction, but it's another thing to continue living out that repentance day after day. Repentance is not a one-time event; it's an ongoing process of turning away from sin and turning toward God. This is why determination is so important—it sustains a person's commitment to repentance over the long haul. In Philippians 3:13-14, Paul writes, "Brethren, I count not myself to have apprehended: but this one thing I do, forgetting those things which are behind, and reaching forth unto those things which are before, I press toward the mark for the prize of the high calling of God in Christ Jesus." Paul's words reflect the determination that is required to continue moving forward in the Christian life, leaving behind the old ways of sin and pressing on toward the goal of living a life that honors God. Repentance requires the same kind of determination—it's about continually pressing forward, even when the journey is difficult.

Determination is also necessary because repentance often involves making sacrifices. When a person repents, they may need to give up certain habits, relationships, or behaviors that are not in line with God's will. This can be painful or difficult, but it is a necessary part of true repentance. Jesus spoke about the cost of discipleship in Luke 14:27, saying, "And whosoever doth not bear his cross, and come after me, cannot be my disciple." Repentance is a part of bearing that cross—it involves a willingness to give up anything that hinders a person's relationship with God. This kind of sacrifice requires strong determination, because the temptation to hold onto those things can be strong. But a person who is truly repentant will be determined to let go of anything that stands in the way of their relationship with God, no matter how difficult it may be.

The role of determination in repentance is also seen in the need for accountability. When a person repents, they often need the support and encouragement of others to help them stay on track. Accountability can be a powerful tool in maintaining determination, as it provides a person with the motivation to continue living out their repentance. In James 5:16, it says, "Confess your faults one to another, and pray one for another, that ye may be healed." By confessing sins to one another and seeking the support of fellow believers, a person can find the strength and determination to continue on the path of repentance. Accountability helps a person stay focused on their commitment to change, and it provides a sense of community and encouragement turn that can strengthen their determination.

Ultimately, the determination required for repentance is not something that a person must muster up on their own. It is God who gives the strength and resolve to follow through on the commitment to change. In Philippians 2:13, it says, "For it is God which worketh in you both to will and to do of his good pleasure." God works in the hearts of those who repent, giving them the determination to live according to His will. Repentance is a partnership between a person's decision to turn from sin and God's empowering grace that enables them to follow through on that decision. Without God's help, the determination required for repentance would be impossible to sustain. But with God's help, a person can have the strength and resolve to live out their repentance, no matter what challenges or temptations they may face.

In conclusion, repentance requires strong determination to follow through on the commitment to change. It's not enough to simply feel sorry for past sins; true repentance is proven through actions, as Paul emphasized in Acts 26:20, where he spoke of the need to "do works meet for repentance." Similarly, Peter's call to the crowd in Acts 2:38 to "repent and be baptized" was not just a call for a momentary decision, but for a life-changing commitment that would require determination to live out. Repentance is a process, one that requires a person to continually turn away from sin and to follow God's ways. This process can be difficult, as it involves breaking free from old habits, facing opposition, making sacrifices, and staying the course over time. But with strong determination, empowered by God's grace, a person can follow through on their commitment to repentance and live a life that reflects true change. Determination is what sustains a person's repentance, enabling them to press on toward the goal of living a life that honors God and brings glory to His name.

Chapter 4 - Dread of Sin

The dread of sin is a powerful force that often drives repentance, causing a person to feel deep sorrow for their wrongdoing and a fear of the consequences that follow. In the Bible, this sense of dread and sorrow over sin is frequently described as a necessary part of true repentance, a sorrow that comes from recognizing the seriousness of sin and its impact on one's relationship with God. David's heartfelt confession in Psalm 38:18 reflects this perfectly: "For I will declare mine iniquity; I will be sorry for my sin." David, a man after God's own heart, was deeply aware of his sin and the grief it caused him. His sorrow was not a shallow regret or a casual acknowledgment of wrongdoing—it was a profound, soul-deep sorrow that came from understanding the weight of his sin and the damage it had caused both in his life and in his relationship with God. David's declaration of his iniquity was not just a statement of fact; it was a cry of deep remorse and regret, a recognition of the seriousness of his offense against a holy and righteous God. This kind of sorrow is an essential part of true repentance because it reflects a heart that is truly broken over sin, a heart that sees sin for what it really is: a destructive force that separates us from God and leads to spiritual death.

The dread of sin is also closely connected to a fear of its consequences. Throughout the Bible, we see examples of people who were warned of the consequences of their sin, and in many cases, this fear of destruction or punishment was what led them to repentance. One of the most striking examples of this is found in the story of Jonah and the city of Nineveh. In Jonah 3:4, Jonah delivers a message from God to the people of Nineveh: "And Jonah began to enter into the city a day's journey, and he cried, and said, Yet forty days, and Nineveh shall be overthrown." Jonah's message was a warning of impending destruction, a clear statement that the people's sin had reached a point where God's judgment was about to fall upon them. The fear of this impending judgment gripped the hearts of the people, and they responded with repentance, turning away from their wicked ways and seeking God's mercy. The dread of sin's consequences drove them to change, and as a result, God spared them from the destruction they had been warned about. This shows us that the fear of sin's consequences can be a powerful motivator for repentance, causing people to recognize the seriousness of their sin and to seek God's forgiveness before it is too late.

The dread of sin is not just about fear of punishment, though. It is also about recognizing the harm that sin causes in our lives and in the lives of those around us. Sin is not just a personal failure or mistake—it is a destructive force that leads to brokenness, pain, and separation from God. David understood this well, and his sorrow over his sin was not just about the fear of punishment but about the recognition of the damage his sin had caused. In Psalm 51:3-4, David says, "For I acknowledge my transgressions: and my sin is ever before me. Against thee, thee only, have I sinned, and done this evil in thy sight." David's grief over his sin was rooted in the realization that he had sinned against God, the One who loved him and had given him everything. His sin had damaged his relationship with God, and this was what caused him the most sorrow. The dread of sin, then, is not just about the fear of punishment—it is about recognizing the deep spiritual harm that sin causes and feeling a deep sorrow over the way it separates us from God.

This deep sorrow over sin is often what leads a person to repentance. When someone truly understands the gravity of their sin and the harm it causes, they are moved to seek God's forgiveness and to turn away from their sinful ways. This sorrow is not the same as worldly sorrow, which is often focused on the consequences of sin for oneself—such as the loss of reputation, the shame of being caught, or the personal pain that sin can cause. Instead, godly sorrow, as described in 2 Corinthians 7:10, leads to repentance: "For godly sorrow worketh repentance to salvation not to be repented of: but the sorrow of the world worketh death." Godly sorrow is a deep, spiritual grief over the fact that sin has grieved the heart of God and has damaged the relationship between the sinner and their Creator. This kind of sorrow leads to true repentance because it is focused on the desire to be reconciled with God and to restore the relationship that sin has damaged.

The dread of sin also includes a recognition of the long-term consequences of unrepentant sin. The Bible is clear that sin leads to death—both physical and spiritual. In Romans 6:23, Paul writes, "For the wages of sin is death; but the gift of God is eternal life through Jesus Christ our Lord." Sin brings destruction, not just in this life but in the life to come. This reality should fill us with a healthy fear of sin, knowing that if we continue in it without repentance, we are choosing the path that leads to death and eternal separation from God. This fear of the ultimate consequences of sin is not meant to paralyze us with terror but to motivate us to turn away from sin and to seek the life that God offers through repentance and faith in Jesus Christ. The dread of sin's consequences, then, is a necessary part of repentance because it helps us to see the urgency of turning away from sin and choosing the path of life.

Another important aspect of the dread of sin is the recognition that sin not only affects the sinner but also has far-reaching consequences for others. Sin often leads to broken relationships, hurt, and harm to those around us. David's sin with Bathsheba, for example, did not just affect him—it led to the death of Uriah, the pain and suffering of Bathsheba, and the eventual death of the child born from their adultery. In Psalm 51, David's sorrow over his sin includes a recognition of the harm he has caused, not just to himself but to others. This recognition of the wider consequences of sin is an important part of the dread of sin because it helps us to see that sin is not just a private matter between us and God—it has the potential to cause great harm to those around us. This should fill us with a healthy fear of sin and motivate us to avoid it, knowing that our actions have consequences not only for ourselves but for others as well.

The dread of sin also involves a deep awareness of the holiness of God and the way in which sin offends His holiness. In Isaiah 6:5, when Isaiah is confronted with a vision of the holiness of God, he cries out, "Woe is me! for I am undone; because I am a man of unclean lips, and I dwell in the midst of a people of unclean lips: for mine eyes have seen the King, the Lord of hosts." Isaiah's encounter with the holiness of God fills him with a deep awareness of his own sinfulness and the sinfulness of the people around him. This awareness of God's holiness is what leads to a true dread of sin, because when we see God for who He really is—pure, holy, and perfect—we begin to understand just how offensive sin is to Him. The closer we draw to God, the more we become aware of His holiness, and the more we become aware of how far short we fall of His perfect standard. This awareness of God's holiness should fill us with a deep dread of sin, because sin is the very thing that separates us from God and offends His perfect nature.

Finally, the dread of sin is also a recognition that sin hinders our ability to experience the fullness of life that God desires for us. Jesus said in John 10:10, "The thief cometh not, but for to steal, and to kill, and to destroy: I am come that they might have life, and that they might have it more abundantly." Sin is like a thief that steals the abundant life that God wants to give us. It leads to spiritual death, brokenness, and separation from God, while repentance leads to life, restoration, and reconciliation with God. The dread of sin, then, is not just about fearing punishment—it is about recognizing that sin robs us of the joy, peace, and fullness of life that God desires for us. When we truly understand this, we begin to see sin for what it really is: a destructive force that we should fear and avoid at all costs.

In conclusion, the dread of sin is an essential part of true repentance. It involves a deep sorrow for sin, as David expressed in Psalm 38:18, where he declared, "I will be sorry for my sin." This sorrow is not just a feeling of regret but a profound recognition of the seriousness of sin and its consequences. The dread of sin also includes a fear of the judgment and destruction that sin brings, as seen in Jonah's warning to the people of Nineveh. But more than that, the dread of sin involves an awareness of the harm that sin causes in our lives, the lives of others, and our relationship with God. It includes a recognition of the holiness of God and the way in which sin offends His perfect nature. And it involves a deep awareness that sin robs us of the abundant life that God desires for us. This dread of sin is what leads us to repentance, causing us to turn away from sin and to seek God's forgiveness and restoration. When we truly understand the seriousness of sin, we are moved to repent with a heart full of sorrow and a determination to live in a way that honors God.

Chapter 5 - Denial of Self

Repentance is a turning point in a person's life, where the decision to follow God's will instead of personal desires takes center stage. One of the key aspects of true repentance is the denial of self, which means putting aside selfish desires and choosing instead to align one's life with the will of God. Jesus made this very clear when He said in Matthew 16:24, "If any man will come after me, let him deny himself, and take up his cross, and follow me." This powerful statement from Jesus highlights that the path of following Him is not an easy one; it requires the denial of self, which involves turning away from our own desires, wants, and ambitions, and instead embracing God's plan for our lives. Denial of self is not just a one-time decision—it is a daily choice that every believer must make as they seek to live a life of repentance. When we repent, we are not merely feeling sorry for our sins, but we are making a commitment to turn away from the selfish desires that led us into sin in the first place. True repentance, therefore, requires a complete shift in our priorities, where God's will becomes the most important thing in our lives.

Self-denial, as taught by Jesus, is essential for anyone who wants to truly follow Him. The phrase "deny himself" means to say no to the things we naturally want in order to say yes to the things God wants for us. This goes against the grain of our human nature, which is often driven by pride, greed, lust, and the desire for control. Denying oneself means giving up these selfish pursuits and instead seeking to live in a way that pleases God. Jesus did not just speak these words without living them out Himself. Throughout His life, Jesus demonstrated the ultimate denial of self by constantly submitting to the will of His Father. In the Garden of Gethsemane, Jesus prayed, "O my Father, if it be possible, let this cup pass from me: nevertheless not as I will, but as thou wilt" Matthew 26:39. Even in the face of immense suffering, Jesus chose to deny His own will and obey the will of His Father. This is the kind of self-denial that true repentance requires. It is a willingness to surrender our own desires, no matter how strong they may be, in order to follow the path that God has laid out for us.

Paul also echoed this theme of repentance and the denial of self when he spoke to the people of Athens in Acts 17:30, saying, "And the times of this ignorance God winked at; but now commandeth all men every where to repent." Paul's call for repentance was not just a call to feel remorse for past mistakes, but a call to turn away from the ways of selfishness and sin and to live a life that aligns with God's will. Repentance, according to Paul, is not optional—it is a command from God for all people. This means that every person, regardless of their background, culture, or personal beliefs, is called to repent and deny themselves in order to live in obedience to God. The denial of self is a necessary part of repentance because it is only by putting aside our own desires that we can truly follow God's will for our lives. Without self-denial, repentance is incomplete, because true repentance requires not just a change of heart but a change of behavior that reflects a new commitment to live according to God's Word.

The concept of denying oneself is difficult for many people because it goes against the natural human instinct to prioritize self-interest. From a young age, we are taught to look out for ourselves, to pursue our own happiness, and to seek our own desires. But Jesus calls us to a different way of living. He calls us to deny ourselves, to give up our own desires for the sake of following Him. This does not mean that our desires are inherently wrong, but it means that we must be willing to submit those desires to God's will. If our desires conflict with what God wants for us, we must be willing to let them go. This is where the true challenge of self-denial comes in—it requires humility and a willingness to trust that God's plans are better than our own.

When we repent, we are essentially making a decision to follow God's will rather than our own. This requires us to acknowledge that our way of living, which was driven by selfish desires, is not the right way. Repentance involves turning away from that old way of living and choosing instead to live according to God's ways. This process of turning away from self and turning toward God is what it means to deny oneself. It is a daily commitment to put aside our own desires and to seek God's will in every area of our lives. This kind of repentance is not easy, because it requires us to let go of the things that we often hold dear.

But Jesus makes it clear that if we want to follow Him, we must be willing to make this sacrifice.

The denial of self also means putting God's will above our own comfort and convenience. Many times, following God's will requires us to step out of our comfort zones and to do things that are difficult or uncomfortable. It may mean giving up certain habits, relationships, or lifestyles that are not in line with God's plan for our lives. It may mean making sacrifices in order to serve others or to live in a way that honors God. But when we deny ourselves in this way, we are demonstrating true repentance, because we are showing that we are no longer living for ourselves but for God. In Luke 9:23, Jesus says, "If any man will come after me, let him deny himself, and take up his cross daily, and follow me." The cross represents sacrifice and suffering, and taking up the cross means being willing to endure whatever challenges come our way in order to follow Jesus. This is the ultimate expression of self-denial—being willing to give up everything, even our own lives, for the sake of following Christ.

Self-denial is not only about giving up sinful desires; it is also about giving up good things if they stand in the way of God's will. Sometimes, we may have desires that are not inherently sinful, but they are not in line with God's plan for our lives. In these cases, we must be willing to let go of those desires in order to follow God. This requires a deep level of trust in God's goodness and His plan for our lives. It means believing that God knows what is best for us, even when it is difficult to understand. When we deny ourselves in this way, we are demonstrating our faith in God and our commitment to following Him, no matter the cost.

Paul understood this well, and he often spoke about the need for self-denial in the Christian life. In Galatians 2:20, Paul says, "I am crucified with Christ: nevertheless I live; yet not I, but Christ liveth in me: and the life which I now live in the flesh I live by the faith of the Son of God, who loved me, and gave himself for me." Paul's statement reflects the reality of self-denial in the life of a believer. When we repent and come to Christ, we are crucifying our old self, with all its selfish desires, and allowing Christ to live in us. This means that our lives are no longer our own—we are now living for Christ. Self-denial is at the heart of this transformation because it is through denying ourselves that we make room for Christ to live and work in us.

The denial of self also requires us to surrender control of our lives to God. As human beings, we often want to be in control of our own lives, to make our own decisions, and to chart our own course. But repentance involves recognizing that we are not in control—God is. When we deny ourselves, we are acknowledging that God's ways are higher than our ways and that His plan for our lives is better than anything we could come up with on our own. This requires humility and a willingness to let go of our need for control. In Proverbs 3:5-6, it says, "Trust in the Lord with all thine heart; and lean not unto thine own understanding. In all thy ways acknowledge him, and he shall direct thy paths." This verse reminds us that when we deny ourselves and trust in God, He will guide us on the right path.

In conclusion, the denial of self is an essential part of true repentance. When Jesus said, "If any man will come after me, let him deny himself," He was calling us to a life of surrender, where our own desires take a backseat to God's will. Repentance requires us to turn away from our selfish desires and to align our lives with God's plan. This is not an easy process—it requires humility, sacrifice, and a willingness to trust in God's goodness and His plan for our lives. But when we deny ourselves in this way, we are demonstrating our commitment to follow Christ, no matter the cost. Paul's message in Acts 17:30 is a reminder that repentance is not optional—it is a command from God. And true repentance, the kind that leads to transformation, always involves the denial of self. By denying ourselves and choosing to follow God's will, we open the door to the abundant life that God has promised us, a life that is no longer driven by selfish desires but is instead guided by the perfect will of our Heavenly Father.

Chapter 6 - Direction Change

Repentance represents a complete change of direction, a turning away from sin and a turning toward God. It is not just about feeling sorry for past mistakes or regretting wrong actions, but it involves a deliberate and intentional decision to change one's life, to forsake the old ways of sin, and to follow God's path of righteousness. This change of direction is emphasized in Isaiah 55:7, where the prophet calls out, "Let the wicked forsake his way, and the unrighteous man his thoughts: and let him return unto the Lord, and he will have mercy upon him; and to our God, for he will abundantly pardon." In this powerful verse, Isaiah explains that true repentance is not merely about confessing wrongdoing, but about abandoning the sinful ways and thoughts that once controlled us and returning wholeheartedly to God. Forsaking one's way implies a total rejection of the life that was lived in rebellion against God, and a desire to follow His will completely. The change of direction that comes with repentance is not just an outward shift in behavior, but an inner transformation that affects our thoughts, desires, and actions. When we repent, we make the conscious decision to leave behind the path of sin and to walk on the path that leads to life and peace in God.

This call to change direction is not new; it is seen throughout Scripture, as God continually calls His people to turn from their wicked ways and return to Him. One such example is found in 1 Samuel 7:3, where Samuel speaks to the children of Israel, saying, "If ye do return unto the Lord with all your hearts, then put away the strange gods and Ashtaroth from among you, and prepare your hearts unto the Lord, and serve him only: and he will deliver you out of the hand of the Philistines." Samuel's call for repentance was not just a call to confess their sins but a command to change the entire direction of their lives. The people were living in idolatry, following false gods, and engaging in practices that were contrary to the will of God. Samuel urged them to return to the Lord with all their hearts, which required them to forsake the idols and the sinful ways that had led them astray. This kind of repentance, which involves a complete change of direction, is what God desires from us as well. It is not enough to simply acknowledge our sin; we must also take action by turning away from that sin and choosing to follow God's ways.

The idea of repentance as a change of direction is central to the Christian faith because it acknowledges that without a deliberate decision to turn away from sin, we will continue to walk in rebellion against God. Sin, by its very nature, is a path that leads away from God. When we choose to live in sin, we are choosing to walk in a direction that leads us farther and farther from the life that God has planned for us. Repentance, therefore, is the act of stopping, turning around, and heading back toward God. This change of direction is not easy, because it often requires us to confront the things in our lives that are keeping us away from God—whether that be habits, relationships, or ways of thinking that are rooted in selfishness and rebellion. But true repentance demands this kind of radical change, because it is only by turning away from sin that we can fully embrace the life that God has called us to live.

The change of direction that comes with repentance is also a sign of true spiritual growth. When a person repents, they are not only acknowledging that they have been going in the wrong direction, but they are also committing to a new way of life that aligns with God's will. This new direction is characterized by obedience to God's Word, a desire to please Him, and a willingness to forsake anything that stands in the way of following Him. In Ephesians 4:22-24, Paul speaks of this change, saying, "That ye put off concerning the former conversation the old man, which is corrupt according to the deceitful lusts; And be renewed in the spirit of your mind; And that ye put on the new man, which after God is created in righteousness and true holiness." Paul's words reflect the deep transformation that takes place when a person repents and changes direction. It is not just a superficial change, but a renewal of the mind and spirit, where the "old man" of sin is put off, and the "new man" of righteousness is put on. This new direction leads to a life of holiness, where the focus is no longer on satisfying selfish desires, but on living in a way that honors God.

Changing direction through repentance also requires humility. To repent means to admit that the path we were on was wrong and that we need to be corrected. This can be difficult, as it often involves admitting that we have been living in ways that are contrary to God's will. In Proverbs 3:5-6, we are told, "Trust in the Lord with all thine heart; and lean not unto thine own understanding. In all thy ways acknowledge him, and he shall direct thy paths." This verse reminds us that when we repent and change direction, we are placing our trust in God's understanding rather than our own. We are acknowledging that His ways are higher than ours and that we need His guidance to stay on the right path. Repentance requires us to surrender our pride and admit that we cannot find the right way on our own. It is a humble recognition that we need God to lead us and that we must follow His direction if we want to live in accordance with His will.

Another important aspect of repentance as a change of direction is the recognition that this change is not temporary or conditional. True repentance is a lifelong commitment to following God's ways and forsaking the ways of sin. In Luke 9:62, Jesus says, "No man, having put his hand to the plough, and looking back, is fit for the kingdom of God." This statement underscores the seriousness of repentance and the need for unwavering commitment. When we repent and turn toward God, we must not look back longingly at the old life of sin that we have left behind. Instead, we must press forward, continually choosing to follow God's direction, even when it is difficult or when we are tempted to return to our old ways. Repentance is not a one-time event but a daily choice to keep moving in the direction that God has set before us.

The change of direction that comes with repentance is also marked by a renewed sense of purpose. When we were living in sin, our focus was often on ourselves and our own desires. But when we repent and turn to God, our focus shifts from ourselves to Him. We begin to seek His will for our lives and to understand that our purpose is not to serve ourselves but to serve Him. This change of direction brings a new sense of meaning and fulfillment, as we realize that we were created to live for God's glory. In 2 Corinthians 5:15, Paul writes, "And that he died for all, that they which live should not henceforth live unto themselves, but unto him which died for them, and rose again." This verse highlights the change of direction that takes place in the life of a believer. When we repent and follow Christ, we no longer live for ourselves but for Him. Our lives take on a new direction, one that is focused on serving God and fulfilling His purpose for us.

Repentance also involves a change in the way we think. Sin often distorts our thinking, leading us to believe lies about ourselves, about others, and about God. When we repent, we must change not only our outward actions but also our thoughts. Isaiah 55:7 tells us, "Let the wicked forsake his way, and the unrighteous man his thoughts." This means that true repentance involves a complete transformation of our minds, where we reject the sinful thoughts that once dominated our thinking and replace them with the truth of God's Word. This change of direction in our thinking is essential because our thoughts often shape our actions. If we continue to entertain sinful thoughts, we will eventually act on them. But if we allow God to renew our minds, we will begin to think in ways that align with His will, and this will lead to actions that are pleasing to Him.

The change of direction that comes with repentance also brings freedom. When we are living in sin, we are often enslaved by our desires and by the patterns of behavior that have taken hold of our lives. But when we repent and turn to God, we are set free from the bondage of sin. In Romans 6:18, Paul writes, "Being then made free from sin, ye became the servants of righteousness." This freedom is not a freedom to do whatever we want, but a freedom to live in righteousness, no longer bound by the chains of sin. The change of direction that comes with repentance leads us away from the path of slavery to sin and toward the path of freedom in Christ. It is a freedom that allows us to live the way God intended us to live, in obedience to His will and in harmony with His purposes.

In conclusion, repentance represents a complete change of direction—from following sin to following God. This change is not just an outward shift in behavior but an inner transformation that affects every aspect of our lives, including our thoughts, desires, and actions. Isaiah 55:7 reminds us that true repentance involves forsaking our wicked ways and turning wholeheartedly to God. Samuel's call to the people of Israel in 1 Samuel 7:3 echoes this, as he urged them to return to the Lord with all their hearts. Repentance requires humility, as we acknowledge that our own way of living was wrong and that we need to be corrected. It also requires commitment, as we choose to follow God's path and not look back to the old life of sin. The change of direction that comes with repentance brings freedom, purpose, and a renewed sense of meaning as we begin to live for God rather than for ourselves. Ultimately, repentance is not just about turning away from sin; it is about turning toward God and embracing the life that He has called us to live.

Chapter 7 - Devotion to God

A life of repentance is deeply rooted in devotion to God, and this devotion is a reflection of a heart that is fully committed to turning away from sin and aligning itself with God's will. True repentance is not just about feeling sorry for wrongdoings; it involves a complete shift in focus, a change in priorities, and a sincere effort to live a life that honors God. Colossians 3:2 says, "Set your affection on things above, not on things on the earth." This verse highlights the essence of devotion to God in a life of repentance. When a person repents, they are making a conscious decision to no longer be consumed with worldly desires and temptations, but instead to fix their heart and mind on the things of God. This act of setting one's affection on things above is an expression of devotion, where the focus of life shifts from earthly pleasures and distractions to a desire to please and honor God in all things. Repentance is a turning away from sin, but it is also a turning toward God, and that turning involves a deep and lasting commitment to live in a way that reflects God's character and commands.

Devotion to God is the natural result of genuine repentance because repentance involves recognizing the seriousness of sin and the way it separates us from God. When a person truly repents, they realize that sin has damaged their relationship with God, and this realization leads to a desire to restore that relationship through renewed devotion. This devotion is not just about going through the motions of religious activity; it is about a heartfelt commitment to seek God, to obey His Word, and to live in a way that honors Him. In Ezekiel 18:30, God, through the prophet, calls the people of Israel to repentance with these words: "Therefore I will judge you, O house of Israel, every one according to his ways, saith the Lord God. Repent, and turn yourselves from all your transgressions; so iniquity shall not be your ruin." This call to repentance was not just about avoiding punishment—it was a call to return to a life of devotion to God, to turn away from the sinful practices that had led them astray, and to recommit themselves to living in obedience to God's commands. In the same way, when we repent, we are not just seeking to escape the consequences of our sins; we are seeking to return to a place of fellowship with God, where our lives are marked by devotion and obedience to Him.

One of the key aspects of devotion to God in a life of repentance is the willingness to forsake anything that stands in the way of our relationship with Him. When we repent, we are making a deliberate decision to put God first in our lives, above all else. This means that we must be willing to let go of the things that distract us from following Him fully—whether those things are sinful behaviors, unhealthy relationships, or worldly desires that pull our attention away from God. Jesus spoke about this kind of devotion in Matthew 6:33, where He said, "But seek ye first the kingdom of God, and his righteousness; and all these things shall be added unto you." Seeking God's kingdom first is an act of devotion that reflects a heart that has truly repented. It means prioritizing God's will above our own desires and trusting that when we put Him first, everything else will fall into place. This kind of devotion requires a shift in focus, where the things of God take precedence over the things of this world.

Repentance is also a process of continually renewing our devotion to God. Just as Ezekiel called the people of Israel to turn from their transgressions and return to God, repentance is not a one-time event but an ongoing journey of devotion. There will be times when we stumble, when we fall short of God's standards, but repentance allows us to realign our hearts with God's will and to renew our commitment to live for Him. In Lamentations 3:22-23, it says, "It is of the Lord's mercies that we are not consumed, because his compassions fail not. They are new every morning: great is thy faithfulness." God's mercies are new every morning, and this truth gives us the assurance that when we repent, we can experience His forgiveness and continue to grow in our devotion to Him. Repentance is not about achieving perfection; it is about continually turning our hearts toward God and seeking to live in a way that pleases Him.

Devotion to God in a life of repentance also involves a commitment to obedience. Repentance is not just about saying we are sorry for our sins; it is about making a decision to live in obedience to God's Word. In John 14:15, Jesus said, "If ye love me, keep my commandments." True devotion to God is demonstrated through obedience to His commands. When we repent, we are making a commitment to follow God's ways rather than our own. This means that we must not only turn away from sin, but we must also actively pursue righteousness. Obedience is the evidence of our devotion to God, and it is through obedience that we show that our repentance is genuine. In James 1:22, we are told, "But be ye doers of the word, and not hearers only, deceiving your own selves." This verse reminds us that true devotion to God is not just about hearing His Word but about putting it into practice in our daily lives. Repentance that leads to devotion is not passive; it is active, involving a daily commitment to live according to God's Word.

Another important aspect of devotion to God in a life of repentance is the pursuit of holiness. When we repent, we are not only turning away from sin, but we are also turning toward a life of holiness, where our thoughts, actions, and desires are aligned with God's will. In 1 Peter 1:15-16, it says, "But as he which hath called you is holy, so be ye holy in all manner of conversation; Because it is written, Be ye holy; for I am holy." Holiness is the natural outgrowth of a life of repentance because repentance involves a desire to be set apart for God's purposes. When we repent, we are committing to live in a way that reflects God's holiness, where our lives are characterized by purity, righteousness, and a desire to honor God in all that we do. This pursuit of holiness is not about trying to earn God's favor, but about responding to His grace by living in a way that pleases Him. Devotion to God means seeking to live a holy life, where our actions and attitudes are in line with God's character.

Devotion to God in a life of repentance also involves a heart of worship. When we repent, we are turning away from the idols of our hearts—the things that we have placed above God—and we are returning to a place of worship, where God is given the honor and glory that He deserves. In Psalm 51:17, David expresses this heart of worship in his prayer of repentance, saying, "The sacrifices of God are a broken spirit: a broken and a contrite heart, O God, thou wilt not despise." True repentance involves a heart that is broken over sin and fully devoted to worshiping God. This kind of worship is not just about singing songs or going through religious rituals; it is about offering our lives as a living sacrifice to God, where every part of our lives is an expression of our devotion to Him. In Romans 12:1, Paul writes, "I beseech you therefore, brethren, by the mercies of God, that ye present your bodies a living sacrifice, holy, acceptable unto God, which is your reasonable service." Devotion to God means living in a way that honors Him, where every decision, every action, and every thought is an act of worship.

Repentance also leads to devotion through a desire for intimacy with God. When we repent, we are acknowledging that sin has created a distance between us and God, and we are seeking to restore that relationship through devotion. In James 4:8, it says, "Draw nigh to God, and he will draw nigh to you. Cleanse your hands, ye sinners; and purify your hearts, ye double minded." This verse reminds us that repentance brings us closer to God, and as we draw near to Him, He draws near to us. Devotion to God is not just about obeying His commands; it is about cultivating a deep and intimate relationship with Him, where we seek His presence and desire to know Him more. Repentance opens the door to this kind of intimacy because it removes the barriers that sin has created and allows us to experience the fullness of God's love and grace.

Finally, devotion to God in a life of repentance is characterized by perseverance. Repentance is not a one-time act; it is a lifelong commitment to following God and staying devoted to Him, even when it is difficult. In Hebrews 12:1, it says, "Wherefore seeing we also are compassed about with so great a cloud of witnesses, let us lay aside every weight, and the sin which doth so easily beset us, and let us run with patience the race that is set before us." This verse reminds us that devotion to God requires perseverance, where we continually lay aside the sin that tries to entangle us and press on in our commitment to follow God. Repentance is a daily act of devotion, where we choose to turn away from sin and to keep our focus on God, no matter what challenges or temptations we may face.

In conclusion, a life of repentance reflects devotion to God, as seen in Colossians 3:2, which calls us to "set our affection on things above, not on things on the earth." Repentance is not just about turning away from sin; it is about turning toward God and committing to live a life that honors Him. Like Ezekiel's call to Israel to turn from their transgressions and return to God, repentance is a call to renewed devotion, where our hearts are fully committed to following God's ways. This devotion is expressed through obedience, holiness, worship, and a desire for intimacy with God. It is a lifelong journey of continually turning our hearts toward God and seeking to live in a way that reflects His love and grace. True repentance leads to a life of devotion, where we are no longer focused on the things of this world, but where our hearts and minds are set on the things of God, and where our greatest desire is to live in a way that brings glory to His name.

Chapter 8 - Deep Humility

Humility is a foundational aspect of repentance, a posture of the heart where a person recognizes their need for God's mercy and grace. Without humility, repentance is incomplete, because it is humility that brings a person to the point of acknowledging their sins and their inability to save themselves. It is through humility that a person can truly understand the depth of their need for God and His forgiveness. In 2 Chronicles 7:14, God speaks to Solomon and gives a powerful promise: "If my people, which are called by my name, shall humble themselves, and pray, and seek my face, and turn from their wicked ways; then will I hear from heaven, and will forgive their sin, and will heal their land." This verse shows that humility is the first step in the process of repentance. It is only when God's people humble themselves, admitting their need for Him, that they can begin to pray, seek His face, and turn from their wicked ways. Humility opens the door to repentance because it leads a person to acknowledge their brokenness and their need for God's intervention.

Humility is essential in repentance because it removes the barriers of pride that often keep people from turning to God. Pride says, "I can handle my problems on my own" or "I don't need God," but humility recognizes that without God, there is no hope. Humility brings a person to the point where they can say, like the tax collector in Luke 18:13, "God be merciful to me a sinner." The tax collector, standing far off, would not even lift his eyes to heaven because he was so aware of his sinfulness. His humble cry for mercy was an expression of true repentance, and Jesus praised his humility, saying in Luke 18:14, "For every one that exalteth himself shall be abased; and he that humbleth himself shall be exalted." This story illustrates the truth that humility is at the heart of repentance. When a person humbles themselves before God, admitting their sin and asking for mercy, they are on the path to forgiveness and restoration.

Humility also involves recognizing that God is the ultimate authority and that His ways are higher than our ways. This is what Elijah urged the people of Israel to understand when he confronted them on Mount Carmel. In 1 Kings 18:21, Elijah asked the people, "How long halt ye between two opinions? if the Lord be God, follow him: but if Baal, then follow him." The people were divided, torn between following the false god Baal and the true God of Israel. Elijah's question was a call for them to humble themselves, to admit that they had been wrong in following Baal, and to return to the Lord. Repentance requires this kind of humility, where a person acknowledges that they have been following the wrong path and that they need to return to God. The people of Israel were hesitant to answer Elijah because admitting their mistake would require humility, but without that humility, they could not experience true repentance.

Another example of humility in repentance is found in the life of King David. After David sinned by committing adultery with Bathsheba and arranging the death of her husband, he was confronted by the prophet Nathan. Instead of denying his sin or making excuses, David humbled himself and confessed his wrongdoing. In Psalm 51:17, David expresses his repentance, saying, "The sacrifices of God are a broken spirit: a broken and a contrite heart, O God, thou wilt not despise." David's humility is evident in his brokenness over his sin. He recognized that what God desired from him was not outward sacrifices but a humble heart that acknowledged his need for forgiveness. David's humility allowed him to repent fully, and because of that, he experienced God's mercy and grace.

In 2 Chronicles 7:14, the call to humility is not just an individual command but a collective one. God speaks to His people as a whole, calling them to humble themselves and seek His face. This shows that humility is not only necessary for personal repentance but also for corporate repentance. When a nation, a church, or a community turns away from God, it requires humility on the part of the whole group to admit their need for God's mercy and to return to Him. This kind of corporate humility is seen in the story of Jonah and the people of Nineveh. When Jonah preached God's message of judgment to Nineveh, the king and the people responded with humility and repentance. In Jonah 3:5-6, it says, "So the people of Nineveh believed God, and proclaimed a fast, and put on sackcloth, from the greatest of them even to the least of them.

For word came unto the king of Nineveh, and he arose from his throne, and he laid his robe from him, and covered him with sackcloth, and sat in ashes." The king of Nineveh humbled himself, removing his royal robes and sitting in ashes as a sign of repentance. His humility, along with the humility of the people, led to God's mercy and the sparing of their city.

Humility in repentance also involves surrendering control to God. Often, people resist repentance because they want to maintain control over their own lives. They do not want to admit that they need God or that they need to change their ways. But true repentance requires a person to humble themselves and give up their desire for control. In James 4:10, we are told, "Humble yourselves in the sight of the Lord, and he shall lift you up." This verse reminds us that when we humble ourselves before God, He will lift us up. But in order to experience that lifting, we must first be willing to bow low before Him, admitting that we cannot save ourselves and that we need His help.

Humility also requires a willingness to be corrected. When a person repents, they are admitting that they were wrong and that they need to change. This requires a heart that is open to correction, a heart that is willing to listen to God's Word and to respond in obedience. In Proverbs 3:11-12, it says, "My son, despise not the chastening of the Lord; neither be weary of his correction: For whom the Lord loveth he correcteth; even as a father the son in whom he delighteth." Humility allows a person to accept God's correction with grace, knowing that His discipline is for their good. When we humble ourselves and accept God's correction, we are showing that we trust Him and that we are willing to follow His ways, even when it is difficult.

Another aspect of humility in repentance is the willingness to forgive others. Just as we need God's mercy, we must also be willing to extend mercy to those who have wronged us. In Matthew 6:14-15, Jesus says, "For if ye forgive men their trespasses, your heavenly Father will also forgive you: But if ye forgive not men their trespasses, neither will your Father forgive your trespasses." Humility in repentance means recognizing that we are not perfect and that we need forgiveness, and therefore, we must also be willing to forgive others. A proud heart holds onto grudges and refuses to forgive, but a humble heart is quick to forgive, knowing that forgiveness is a reflection of God's grace.

Humility is also seen in the willingness to confess sins openly. In 1 John 1:9, it says, "If we confess our sins, he is faithful and just to forgive us our sins, and to cleanse us from all unrighteousness." Confession requires humility because it involves admitting our failures and mistakes. It is often tempting to hide our sins or to pretend that everything is fine, but true repentance involves bringing our sins into the light and asking for God's forgiveness. When we confess our sins, we are acknowledging that we cannot fix the problem on our own and that we need God's cleansing and forgiveness.

Humility in repentance is also reflected in a heart that is willing to serve others. In Philippians 2:3-4, Paul writes, "Let nothing be done through strife or vainglory; but in lowliness of mind let each esteem other better than themselves. Look not every man on his own things, but every man also on the things of others." A humble heart is one that is focused on serving others rather than seeking its own glory. Repentance involves turning away from selfishness and pride and embracing a life of humility and service. When we humble ourselves and serve others, we are reflecting the character of Christ, who "made himself of no reputation, and took upon him the form of a servant" Philippians 2:7.

In conclusion, deep humility is a key aspect of repentance. As seen in 2 Chronicles 7:14, repentance begins with humility, where God's people are called to humble themselves, pray, seek His face, and turn from their wicked ways. Humility involves recognizing our need for God's mercy, surrendering control to Him, being open to correction, and being willing to forgive others. It also involves confessing our sins openly and serving others with a heart of humility. Elijah's call to Israel in 1 Kings 18:21 was a call to humility, urging the people to choose between following God or following Baal. Repentance requires this same kind of humility, where we choose to turn away from our pride and self-reliance and instead submit ourselves fully to God. When we humble ourselves before God in repentance, we open the door to His mercy, forgiveness, and healing.

Chapter 9 - Deliverance from Sin

Repentance brings deliverance from the bondage of sin, a powerful truth that is central to the message of the Bible. When a person repents, they turn away from sin and toward God, and in doing so, they are set free from the chains that sin has placed upon them. Jesus Himself emphasized this when He said in John 8:36, "If the Son therefore shall make you free, ye shall be free indeed." This statement highlights the fact that true freedom comes only through Jesus Christ. Sin, by its very nature, binds and enslaves a person, trapping them in destructive patterns of behavior and separating them from the life that God desires for them. But through repentance, and by turning to Jesus, a person can experience true deliverance—freedom from the power and consequences of sin.

Sin is a form of bondage because it takes control of a person's life, leading them to act in ways that are harmful to themselves and others. It distorts their thinking, causes them to make poor decisions, and ultimately leads to spiritual death. In Romans 6:23, Paul writes, "For the wages of sin is death; but the gift of God is eternal life through Jesus Christ our Lord." This verse makes it clear that the final outcome of a life lived in sin is death—both physical and spiritual. Sin leads to separation from God, and this separation is the ultimate form of bondage. However, repentance opens the door to deliverance because it allows a person to turn away from this path of destruction and instead receive the gift of eternal life through Jesus Christ. Repentance, then, is the first step toward freedom because it involves acknowledging the bondage of sin and seeking God's help to break free.

The deliverance that comes through repentance is not just about being set free from the consequences of sin; it is also about being set free from the power of sin. Before a person repents, they are often trapped in patterns of sinful behavior that they cannot break on their own. These patterns may include things like addiction, anger, dishonesty, or selfishness. Sin becomes a habit, a way of life that is difficult to escape. But when a person repents and turns to God, He gives them the strength to break free from these patterns. In 1 Corinthians 10:13, Paul writes, "There hath no temptation taken you but such as is common to man: but God is faithful, who will not suffer you to be tempted above that ye are able; but will with the temptation also make a way to escape, that ye may be able to bear it." This verse reassures us that God will provide a way out of temptation, and repentance is the first step in finding that way out. When we repent, we are no longer under the control of sin; instead, we are under the control of God's grace, which empowers us to live in righteousness.

The deliverance that repentance brings is also exemplified in the story of Moses and the children of Israel. In Deuteronomy 30:2, Moses called the people of Israel to repentance, saying, "And shalt return unto the Lord thy God, and shalt obey his voice according to all that I command thee this day, thou and thy children, with all thine heart, and with all thy soul." This call to return to the Lord was an invitation to experience deliverance, both spiritually and physically. The people of Israel had repeatedly fallen into sin and rebellion against God, and as a result, they faced many hardships, including captivity and oppression. But Moses reminded them that if they would turn back to God with all their heart and soul, they would experience His deliverance. This deliverance was not just from their physical enemies, but from the spiritual bondage that had come as a result of their disobedience. In the same way, when we repent and turn to God, we experience deliverance from the spiritual bondage that sin has brought into our lives. We are set free from the guilt, shame, and consequences of our past mistakes, and we are given a new opportunity to live in the freedom that God offers.

Deliverance from sin through repentance is also about experiencing a new identity in Christ. When a person repents and accepts Jesus as their Savior, they are no longer defined by their past sins. Instead, they are given a new identity as a child of God. In 2 Corinthians 5:17, Paul writes, "Therefore if any man be in Christ, he is a new creature: old things are passed away; behold, all things are become new." This verse speaks to the transformative power of repentance. When we repent, we are not just forgiven for our sins; we are made new. The old life of sin and bondage is gone, and we are given a fresh start in Christ. This new identity is one of freedom and victory, where we are no longer slaves to sin but are empowered to live according to God's will.

Another important aspect of deliverance from sin through repentance is the role of the Holy Spirit. When a person repents and turns to God, the Holy Spirit comes to dwell within them, giving them the power to overcome sin and live a life that is pleasing to God. In Romans 8:9, Paul writes, "But ye are not in the flesh, but in the Spirit, if so be that the Spirit of God dwell in you. Now if any man have not the Spirit of Christ, he is none of his." The presence of the Holy Spirit in the life of a believer is evidence of their deliverance from sin. The Holy Spirit guides, convicts, and strengthens the believer, helping them to resist temptation and to walk in obedience to God's Word. Repentance opens the door to this relationship with the Holy Spirit, and it is through His power that we are able to experience true deliverance from the bondage of sin.

The deliverance that repentance brings is also a process of sanctification, where a person is continually being transformed into the image of Christ. While repentance brings immediate freedom from the guilt of sin, the process of becoming more like Christ is ongoing. In Philippians 1:6, Paul writes, "Being confident of this very thing, that he which hath begun a good work in you will perform it until the day of Jesus Christ." This verse reminds us that God is continually working in the lives of those who have repented, helping them to grow in their faith and to live in greater freedom from sin. Sanctification is the process by which a person is made holy, and it is a lifelong journey that begins with repentance. As we continue to repent of our sins and seek God's guidance, we experience greater levels of deliverance and freedom in our lives.

Repentance also brings deliverance from the fear of judgment. Before a person repents, they may live in fear of God's judgment because they know that their sins have separated them from Him. But when a person repents and turns to Jesus, they no longer have to fear judgment because Jesus has taken the punishment for their sins. In Romans 8:1, it says, "There is therefore now no condemnation to them which are in Christ Jesus, who walk not after the flesh, but after the Spirit." This verse is a powerful reminder that repentance brings deliverance from the fear of condemnation. When we repent, we are no longer under God's wrath; instead, we are under His grace. We can live in peace, knowing that our sins have been forgiven and that we are no longer condemned.

Deliverance from sin through repentance also brings peace and joy into a person's life. Sin creates turmoil, guilt, and unrest in a person's heart, but repentance brings peace because it restores a person's relationship with God. In Romans 5:1, Paul writes, "Therefore being justified by faith, we have peace with God through our Lord Jesus Christ." This peace comes from knowing that we are forgiven and that we are in right standing with God. Along with peace, repentance brings joy, because there is great joy in knowing that we have been set free from the bondage of sin and that we are now walking in the light of God's grace. In Luke 15:7, Jesus says, "I say unto you, that likewise joy shall be in heaven over one sinner that repenteth, more than over ninety and nine just persons, which need no repentance." The joy that comes from repentance is not only experienced by the repentant sinner but also by all of heaven. This joy is a reflection of the freedom and deliverance that repentance brings.

In conclusion, repentance brings deliverance from the bondage of sin. Jesus said in John 8:36, "If the Son therefore shall make you free, ye shall be free indeed." This deliverance is seen throughout Scripture, including in Moses' call for the people of Israel to return to the Lord for deliverance, as found in Deuteronomy 30:2. Through repentance, a person is set free from the power and consequences of sin, and they are given a new identity in Christ. The Holy Spirit empowers them to live in freedom, guiding them in the process of sanctification. Repentance also brings deliverance from the fear of judgment, as those who repent are no longer under condemnation but are justified by faith. Along with deliverance, repentance brings peace and joy, as the repentant sinner experiences the freedom of being forgiven and restored to a right relationship with God. True deliverance from sin can only come through repentance and faith in Jesus Christ, and it is through Him that we are set free to live the life that God has called us to live.

Chapter 10 - Divine Forgiveness

Divine forgiveness is one of the most profound and gracious gifts that God offers to humanity, and it is available to all who come to Him in genuine repentance. Repentance opens the door to divine forgiveness, as is beautifully expressed in 1 John 1:9, where it says, "If we confess our sins, he is faithful and just to forgive us our sins, and to cleanse us from all unrighteousness." This verse assures us that no matter what sins we have committed, no matter how far we may have strayed from God, if we are willing to confess our sins and repent, God is faithful and just to forgive us. He does not hold our sins against us once we have repented; instead, He wipes them away and offers us a fresh start. This promise of divine forgiveness is a reflection of God's incredible mercy and love for His people. When we come to Him in humility, acknowledging our wrongdoing, He is always ready to forgive and cleanse us from all unrighteousness. Repentance is the key that unlocks the door to this forgiveness, and without it, we remain separated from the full experience of God's grace.

One of the most compelling examples of divine forgiveness is seen in the book of Jeremiah, where God, through the prophet, pleads with backsliding Israel to return to Him. In Jeremiah 3:12, God says, "Go and proclaim these words toward the north, and say, Return, thou backsliding Israel, saith the Lord; and I will not cause mine anger to fall upon you: for I am merciful, saith the Lord, and I will not keep anger for ever." This passage reveals God's heart of mercy and His readiness to forgive even those who have turned their backs on Him. Israel had repeatedly sinned against God, worshiping idols and rejecting His commandments, but despite their unfaithfulness, God still desired to forgive them. He called them to repentance, promising that if they would return to Him, He would not pour out His anger upon them but would instead extend His mercy. This shows that divine forgiveness is not something that God withholds from those who have fallen into sin; rather, it is something that He offers freely to all who are willing to repent and return to Him. God's forgiveness is not limited to those who have lived perfect lives; it is available to everyone, even those who have made serious mistakes, as long as they are willing to come to Him in repentance.

The concept of divine forgiveness is woven throughout the entire Bible, from the Old Testament to the New Testament, and it consistently reveals the depth of God's love and compassion for His people. In Psalm 103:12, it says, "As far as the east is from the west, so far hath he removed our transgressions from us." This verse illustrates the completeness of God's forgiveness. When we repent and seek His forgiveness, He does not merely overlook our sins or sweep them under the rug; He removes them completely, casting them as far away from us as the east is from the west. This means that our sins are no longer held against us, and we are no longer defined by them. Through divine forgiveness, we are given a new identity, one that is rooted in God's grace rather than in our past mistakes.

Divine forgiveness is also a reflection of God's justice. In 1 John 1:9, we are told that God is both "faithful and just" to forgive us our sins. This means that God's forgiveness is not arbitrary or unfair; it is rooted in His perfect justice. Because Jesus Christ paid the price for our sins on the cross, God is able to forgive us in a way that upholds His justice. Jesus took the punishment that we deserved, and because of His sacrifice, we are able to receive forgiveness when we repent. This shows that divine forgiveness is not something that we earn through our own efforts or good deeds; it is a gift that is made possible by the work of Christ. Repentance is simply the means by which we receive this gift. When we confess our sins and turn away from them, we are acknowledging our need for God's mercy and accepting the forgiveness that has already been made available to us through Jesus.

The story of the prodigal son in Luke 15 is another powerful example of divine forgiveness. In this parable, Jesus tells the story of a young man who demands his inheritance from his father and then goes off to a far country, where he wastes all his money on sinful living. Eventually, he finds himself in a desperate situation, feeding pigs and longing for food, and he realizes that he has sinned against both his father and God. In humility, he decides to return to his father and repent, saying, "Father, I have sinned against heaven, and before thee, and am no more worthy to be called thy son" Luke 15:21. But instead of condemning his son or rejecting him, the father runs to him, embraces him, and forgives him completely. This parable illustrates the depth of God's forgiveness. No matter how far we have wandered from Him, no matter how badly we have sinned, when we repent and return to Him, He is always ready to forgive us and welcome us back into His family. The father's embrace of the prodigal son is a picture of divine forgiveness, where God not only forgives our sins but restores us to a place of honor and love in His kingdom.

The Bible also teaches that divine forgiveness is not just about being forgiven for our past sins; it is also about being cleansed from all unrighteousness. When we repent, God not only forgives us, but He also cleanses us from the sin that has stained our hearts and lives. In Isaiah 1:18, God says, "Come now, and let us reason together, saith the Lord: though your sins be as scarlet, they shall be as white as snow; though they be red like crimson, they shall be as wool." This verse speaks to the transformative power of divine forgiveness. When we repent, God takes the stains of sin that have marked our lives and washes them away, making us pure and clean in His sight. This cleansing is a vital part of divine forgiveness because it allows us to move forward in our relationship with God without the burden of guilt or shame. Through repentance, we are not only forgiven, but we are also made new, free from the weight of our past sins.

Another important aspect of divine forgiveness is that it is freely given. God does not withhold forgiveness from those who seek it, nor does He make us jump through hoops to earn it. In Isaiah 55:7, it says, "Let the wicked forsake his way, and the unrighteous man his thoughts: and let him return unto the Lord, and he will have mercy upon him; and to our God, for he will abundantly pardon." This verse emphasizes that God's forgiveness is abundant and freely available to all who repent and return to Him. There is no sin too great, no failure too severe, that God's forgiveness cannot cover. He is always ready to extend His mercy to those who humble themselves and seek His grace.

However, while divine forgiveness is freely given, it does require genuine repentance. In Acts 3:19, Peter calls the people to repent, saying, "Repent ye therefore, and be converted, that your sins may be blotted out, when the times of refreshing shall come from the presence of the Lord." This verse shows that repentance is necessary in order for our sins to be blotted out. We must turn away from our sins and turn toward God in order to receive His forgiveness. Repentance is not just about feeling sorry for our sins; it is about making a commitment to change, to leave behind the sinful behaviors and attitudes that have separated us from God. When we do this, God is faithful to forgive us and to restore us to a right relationship with Him.

Divine forgiveness also leads to reconciliation. When we repent and are forgiven by God, we are not only freed from the guilt of our sins, but we are also reconciled to Him. In 2 Corinthians 5:18-19, Paul writes, "And all things are of God, who hath reconciled us to himself by Jesus Christ, and hath given to us the ministry of reconciliation; To wit, that God was in Christ, reconciling the world unto himself, not imputing their trespasses unto them." This reconciliation is the ultimate goal of divine forgiveness. God does not just forgive our sins and leave us to continue living apart from Him; He brings us back into fellowship with Him. Through repentance and forgiveness, we are restored to a relationship with God, where we can experience His love, grace, and peace.

In conclusion, divine forgiveness is one of the most precious gifts that God offers to those who repent. As 1 John 1:9 promises, "If we confess our sins, he is faithful and just to forgive us our sins, and to cleanse us from all unrighteousness." This forgiveness is not something that we earn or deserve; it is a reflection of God's incredible mercy and love. Through repentance, we open the door to this forgiveness, and when we turn to God in humility, He is always ready to forgive us and cleanse us from our sins. This divine forgiveness is also reflected in Jeremiah's plea for backsliding Israel to return to the Lord, showing that God's readiness to forgive extends even to those who have wandered far from Him. When we repent, we not only receive forgiveness for our past sins, but we also experience God's cleansing power, which removes the stain of sin from our lives and allows us to walk in newness of life. Through divine forgiveness, we are reconciled to God, restored to a place of fellowship with Him, and given the freedom to live in His grace and love. This is the beauty of repentance and divine forgiveness, a gift that is available to all who come to God with a humble and repentant heart.

Chapter 11 - Daily Renewal

Repentance is not a one-time event, but a continual process of daily renewal that reflects a lifelong commitment to walking in the ways of God. This idea is vividly expressed by the apostle Paul when he says in 1 Corinthians 15:31, "I protest by your rejoicing which I have in Christ Jesus our Lord, I die daily." Paul's words here show that the Christian life involves a constant turning away from sin and a daily commitment to live for God. This "dying daily" is a form of repentance, where a believer acknowledges their sinful nature and chooses each day to put aside their selfish desires and follow the path that God has laid out for them. It is the recognition that, although we have been forgiven and made new in Christ, the battle against sin and the temptations of the world is ongoing. Each day presents new challenges, new temptations, and new opportunities to either follow God or to fall back into sinful ways. Therefore, daily renewal through repentance is essential for maintaining a close and faithful relationship with God.

The concept of daily renewal through repentance is not just about avoiding sin, but about actively seeking to live in a way that pleases God. This is reflected in the words of the prophet Amos, who in Amos 5:14-15 calls the people of Israel to, "Seek good, and not evil, that ye may live: and so the Lord, the God of hosts, shall be with you, as ye have spoken. Hate the evil, and love the good, and establish judgment in the gate: it may be that the Lord God of hosts will be gracious unto the remnant of Joseph." Amos' call to "seek good" and "hate the evil" reflects the ongoing nature of repentance. It is not enough to simply turn away from evil once; we must continually seek to do good and to align our lives with God's will. This requires daily self-examination, where we look at our actions, thoughts, and desires, and ask whether they are in line with what God wants for us. If we find that we have strayed, repentance allows us to turn back to God, seek His forgiveness, and renew our commitment to living according to His Word.

This process of daily renewal is a key aspect of spiritual growth. As believers, we are called to be conformed to the image of Christ, but this transformation does not happen all at once. Instead, it is a gradual process that takes place over time as we continually turn to God in repentance and allow Him to shape us into the people He wants us to be. In Romans 12:2, Paul writes, "And be not conformed to this world: but be ye transformed by the renewing of your mind, that ye may prove what is that good, and acceptable, and perfect, will of God." The renewal of the mind that Paul speaks of here is closely connected to the idea of daily repentance. As we repent of our sinful thoughts and behaviors, we allow God to transform our minds and hearts, so that we begin to think and act more like Christ. This daily renewal is necessary because the world constantly tries to pull us away from God and conform us to its values. Through repentance, we resist this pressure and instead choose to be shaped by God's truth.

Daily renewal through repentance also involves a constant awareness of our dependence on God's grace. No matter how long we have been following Christ, we never reach a point where we no longer need God's forgiveness and help. Each day, we must come to God in humility, acknowledging our weaknesses and asking for His strength to live in a way that honors Him. In Lamentations 3:22-23, it says, "It is of the Lord's mercies that we are not consumed, because his compassions fail not. They are new every morning: great is thy faithfulness." This verse reminds us that God's mercies are new every day, and we can come to Him each morning with the assurance that He will provide the grace we need to walk in His ways. Repentance is not about living in constant guilt or shame, but about recognizing our need for God's mercy and experiencing His grace afresh each day.

The idea of "dying daily," as Paul describes it, also points to the need for ongoing surrender. Each day, we must make the choice to surrender our will to God's will, to lay down our desires and ambitions and allow God to guide our steps. This daily surrender is a form of repentance because it involves turning away from the pursuit of our own selfish goals and seeking instead to live for God's glory. In Luke 9:23, Jesus says, "If any man will come after me, let him deny himself, and take up his cross daily, and follow me." Taking up the cross daily is a picture of repentance, where we die to ourselves and live for Christ. It is not an easy path, but it is the only path that leads to true life and peace in God.

Daily renewal through repentance also keeps us humble before God. As we recognize our need for continual repentance, we are reminded that we are not perfect and that we rely on God's grace every day. This humility is essential for maintaining a close relationship with God, because pride can easily creep in when we forget our need for repentance. In James 4:6, it says, "God resisteth the proud, but giveth grace unto the humble." By repenting daily and seeking God's help, we remain humble and open to His leading in our lives. Humility also allows us to show grace and forgiveness to others, knowing that we, too, are in need of God's forgiveness.

The daily process of repentance and renewal also has a purifying effect on our hearts. As we repent and turn back to God each day, we allow Him to cleanse us from the impurities of sin that may have crept into our lives. In Psalm 51:10, David prays, "Create in me a clean heart, O God; and renew a right spirit within me." This prayer reflects the desire for daily renewal, where we ask God to cleanse us from anything that is not pleasing to Him and to give us a right spirit. Repentance purifies us because it brings our sins into the light and allows God to wash them away, making us clean and restoring our fellowship with Him.

Daily renewal through repentance also strengthens our faith. As we continually turn to God in repentance, we experience His forgiveness and grace in new ways, which deepens our trust in His faithfulness. Each time we repent, we are reminded that God is patient and merciful, and this strengthens our confidence in His love for us. In 1 John 1:9, we are assured, "If we confess our sins, he is faithful and just to forgive us our sins, and to cleanse us from all unrighteousness." This promise of forgiveness gives us the courage to come to God daily, knowing that He will never turn us away. As we experience His forgiveness again and again, our faith in His goodness and mercy grows stronger.

Daily repentance also helps us to live with a clear conscience before God and others. When we repent regularly, we do not allow sin to build up in our lives, but we deal with it immediately by bringing it before God. This keeps our hearts pure and allows us to live with integrity. In Acts 24:16, Paul says, "And herein do I exercise myself, to have always a conscience void of offence toward God, and toward men." By repenting daily, we maintain a clear conscience and are able to live in peace, knowing that we are walking in right relationship with God and others.

The daily process of renewal through repentance also brings joy. While repentance involves a recognition of our sin and the need for correction, it ultimately leads to joy because it restores our fellowship with God. In Psalm 51:12, David prays, "Restore unto me the joy of thy salvation; and uphold me with thy free spirit." When we repent, we experience the joy of being forgiven and restored to a close relationship with God. This joy is not based on our circumstances, but on the knowledge that we are loved and accepted by God, no matter what.

In addition to bringing personal renewal, daily repentance also has a positive impact on our relationships with others. As we experience God's forgiveness, we are better able to forgive those who have wronged us. Repentance softens our hearts and makes us more compassionate and understanding toward others, because we recognize that we, too, are in need of grace. In Colossians 3:13, it says, "Forbearing one another, and forgiving one another, if any man have a quarrel against any: even as Christ forgave you, so also do ye." Daily repentance allows us to extend the same forgiveness to others that we have received from God, which leads to healthier and more loving relationships.

In conclusion, daily renewal through repentance is an essential part of the Christian life. As Paul says in 1 Corinthians 15:31, we must "die daily," continually turning away from sin and turning toward God. This daily process of repentance is reflected in the words of Amos, who urges us to "seek good, and not evil," and to live rightly before God. Through daily repentance, we experience God's forgiveness and grace afresh each day, which brings renewal to our hearts and minds. It strengthens our faith, purifies our hearts, and allows us to live with a clear conscience. Repentance also keeps us humble, reminding us of our need for God's mercy, and it brings joy as we experience the restoration of our relationship with Him. As we repent daily, we grow in our walk with God and become more conformed to the image of Christ. This ongoing process of daily renewal is a key aspect of spiritual growth and is necessary for living a life that is pleasing to God.

Chapter 12 - Dependence on God's Grace

Repentance reveals our complete dependence on God's grace, underscoring the fact that salvation is not something we can earn or achieve through our own efforts, but is entirely a gift from God. This truth is powerfully expressed in Ephesians 2:8-9, where Paul writes, "For by grace are ye saved through faith; and that not of yourselves: it is the gift of God: Not of works, lest any man should boast." These verses emphasize that it is by God's grace, and not by our own works, that we are saved. Repentance, therefore, is not about trying to earn God's forgiveness by being good enough or doing enough good deeds; instead, it is about recognizing our complete inability to save ourselves and turning to God in humble reliance on His grace. Repentance is an act of surrender, where we acknowledge that we have sinned and fallen short of God's standard, and that our only hope for forgiveness and salvation is found in the grace of God through Jesus Christ. This dependence on God's grace is central to the Christian faith and is the foundation of true repentance.

The concept of grace is woven throughout the entire Bible, and it is always linked to God's love and mercy toward His people. Grace is God's unmerited favor, His willingness to forgive us and restore us to Himself, even though we have done nothing to deserve it. Repentance is the means by which we receive this grace, as it involves turning away from our sins and turning toward God, trusting in His mercy and forgiveness. Isaiah 55:6-7 calls people to seek the Lord and return to Him, saying, "Seek ye the Lord while he may be found, call ye upon him while he is near: Let the wicked forsake his way, and the unrighteous man his thoughts: and let him return unto the Lord, and he will have mercy upon him; and to our God, for he will abundantly pardon." This passage highlights the abundant pardon that God offers to those who repent and seek Him. God's grace is not limited or scarce; it is abundant and overflowing, available to all who come to Him in repentance. This abundance of grace shows that no matter how far we have strayed or how deeply we have sinned, God's grace is more than enough to cover our sins and restore us to a right relationship with Him.

Repentance is, therefore, an act of humility, where we acknowledge that we cannot save ourselves and that we are completely dependent on God's grace. It is a recognition that we are sinners in need of a Savior, and that only through God's grace can we be forgiven and made right with Him. In Romans 3:23-24, Paul writes, "For all have sinned, and come short of the glory of God; Being justified freely by his grace through the redemption that is in Christ Jesus." This verse reminds us that every person has sinned and fallen short of God's glory, but through the grace of God, we are justified—made right with God—through the redemption that comes through Jesus Christ. This justification is not something we can earn through our own efforts; it is a gift of God's grace that is received through repentance and faith in Jesus.

Dependence on God's grace is also seen in the way that repentance brings us into a deeper relationship with God. When we repent, we are turning away from our sins and turning toward God, seeking His forgiveness and His presence in our lives. This act of repentance draws us closer to God, as we recognize our need for His grace and rely on Him to cleanse us from our sins. In James 4:8, it says, "Draw nigh to God, and he will draw nigh to you. Cleanse your hands, ye sinners; and purify your hearts, ye double minded." Repentance is the way in which we draw near to God, and as we do, He draws near to us, extending His grace and mercy to cleanse us and restore us to fellowship with Him. This shows that repentance is not just about turning away from sin; it is about turning toward God and relying on His grace to restore and renew us.

God's grace is also what empowers us to live a transformed life after repentance. When we repent and receive God's grace, we are not only forgiven, but we are also given the strength and power to live in a way that honors God. In Titus 2:11-12, it says, "For the grace of God that bringeth salvation hath appeared to all men, Teaching us that, denying ungodliness and worldly lusts, we should live soberly, righteously, and godly, in this present world." God's grace not only saves us, but it also teaches us how to live. It gives us the ability to deny sin and to live in a way that reflects God's holiness and righteousness. This shows that repentance is not just a one-time event, but a continual process of relying on God's grace to live a life that is pleasing to Him. Every day, we must depend on God's grace to help us resist temptation and to live in obedience to His will.

The dependence on God's grace is further emphasized by the fact that we are unable to repent without God's help. Even the act of repentance itself is a gift of God's grace. In Acts 11:18, it says, "When they heard these things, they held their peace, and glorified God, saying, Then hath God also to the Gentiles granted repentance unto life." This verse shows that repentance is something that God grants to us—it is not something we can muster up on our own. It is by God's grace that we are able to see our need for repentance and turn to Him in faith. This highlights our complete dependence on God, not only for forgiveness but even for the ability to repent. Without God's grace, we would remain in our sins, blind to our need for salvation.

Isaiah's call for the people to seek the Lord while He may be found and to return to Him for abundant pardon (Isaiah 55:6-7) also underscores the urgency of repentance and the availability of God's grace. God is always ready to forgive, but we must seek Him and turn to Him while there is still time. This call to repentance is an invitation to experience the fullness of God's grace, which is available to all who turn to Him. It is a reminder that God's grace is not something we should take for granted, but something we must actively seek through repentance. When we come to God in humility and dependence, He responds with grace, offering us forgiveness and new life in Him.

Another important aspect of our dependence on God's grace is the fact that grace is what sustains us throughout our Christian journey. From the moment we repent and place our faith in Christ, to the daily struggles we face in living a godly life, we are constantly in need of God's grace. In 2 Corinthians 12:9, Paul writes, "And he said unto me, My grace is sufficient for thee: for my strength is made perfect in weakness. Most gladly therefore will I rather glory in my infirmities, that the power of Christ may rest upon me." God's grace is sufficient for every challenge we face, and it is through His grace that we are able to endure trials, resist temptation, and grow in our faith. Repentance is the first step in receiving God's grace, but it is also something we must continue to rely on every day as we seek to live a life that honors Him.

Repentance also reveals our dependence on God's grace in the way it brings about spiritual healing and restoration. Sin damages our relationship with God and with others, but through repentance, God's grace brings healing to those broken relationships. In Psalm 147:3, it says, "He healeth the broken in heart, and bindeth up their wounds." God's grace is the healing balm that restores our hearts and brings wholeness to the areas of our lives that have been wounded by sin. Repentance allows us to receive this healing, as we turn to God and allow Him to work in our hearts, restoring what has been broken and making us whole again.

Finally, dependence on God's grace through repentance is the only way to experience true and lasting peace. Sin creates turmoil and unrest in our hearts, but when we repent and receive God's grace, we experience the peace that comes from knowing we are forgiven and reconciled to God. In Philippians 4:7, Paul writes, "And the peace of God, which passeth all understanding, shall keep your hearts and minds through Christ Jesus." This peace is a gift of God's grace, and it is only available to those who come to Him in repentance and faith. It is a peace that goes beyond our circumstances, because it is rooted in the assurance that we are forgiven, loved, and accepted by God.

In conclusion, repentance shows our complete dependence on God's grace. As Ephesians 2:8-9 reminds us, salvation is a gift of grace, not something we can earn through our own efforts. Isaiah's call to seek the Lord and return to Him for abundant pardon in Isaiah 55:6-7 emphasizes the fact that God's grace is available to all who repent and turn to Him. Repentance is the means by which we receive God's grace, and it reveals our need for His mercy and forgiveness. It is through God's grace that we are forgiven, cleansed, and empowered to live a life that honors Him. Repentance is not a one-time event, but a continual process of turning to God and relying on His grace to sustain us. Each day, we must depend on God's grace to help us resist sin, grow in our faith, and experience the healing and peace that only He can provide. Without God's grace, we would remain in our sins, unable to save ourselves or live in a way that pleases Him. But through repentance and faith in Christ, we can experience the fullness of God's grace and live in the freedom and peace that He offers.

Conclusion

As we come to the end of "Repentance Revealed - The Road Back to God", I hope you have felt the deep and powerful truth that repentance is not something to fear or avoid but a beautiful journey that leads us closer to God. Life has its moments when we stray, when we feel burdened by the weight of our choices or the pressures of this world. But no matter how far we've wandered, God's grace is always available, and the path back to Him is never closed. Repentance is that road, and it's a road paved with mercy, forgiveness, and the incredible love of God, who longs to restore us to the fullness of life He designed for us.

One of the most important truths you can carry with you is that repentance is not a single moment in time. It's not just a response to a big mistake or a crisis of conscience. Instead, it's an ongoing journey, a daily choice to turn toward God and away from the things that pull us in the opposite direction. Paul's words in 1 Corinthians 15:31 remind us that as followers of Christ, we are called to "die daily"—to let go of the selfish desires, sins, and distractions that keep us from living fully in God's will. This daily renewal isn't about being perfect; it's about continually aligning ourselves with God's grace, trusting Him to guide us, and knowing that His mercy is new every morning.

Throughout this book, we've explored what it means to walk the road of repentance. We've looked at how God calls His people, time and again, to return to Him. From the Israelites in the Old Testament to the teachings of Jesus and the apostles, the message is clear: God's heart is for restoration. He doesn't want to condemn or punish us—He wants to forgive, heal, and transform us. Repentance is the doorway through which we step into that transformation, and it's something that brings life, not shame. Consider the words of Isaiah 55:6-7, where God calls us to seek Him while He may be found, to return to Him so that He may "abundantly pardon." This isn't a distant, cold call from a far-off deity. It's a personal, loving invitation from a God who is always ready to forgive. No matter what we've done, no matter how many times we've failed, God's grace is sufficient. Repentance opens the door to that grace, and when we walk through it, we find that God is already there, waiting with open arms.

But as we've seen, repentance isn't just about turning away from sin—it's about turning toward something far greater: a life of joy, peace, and purpose in God. It's about realigning our hearts with His, seeking His will for our lives, and experiencing the freedom that comes from being in right relationship with Him. When we repent, we let go of the burdens of guilt and shame, and we step into the incredible light of God's forgiveness and love. This is the heart of repentance: not looking back in regret, but looking forward to the new life that God promises us in Christ.

If there's one thing I hope you take from this book, it's that repentance is a gift. It's an invitation to start fresh every day, to leave behind the things that weigh us down and keep us from living the abundant life that God has for us. It's not about perfection; it's about progression. It's about growing closer to God, day by day, and allowing Him to shape us into the people He created us to be. Repentance is the key to this journey, and it's available to all of us, no matter where we've been or what we've done.

As you move forward from here, I encourage you to embrace repentance as a daily practice. Let it be a time of reflection, where you come before God with honesty, acknowledging the areas where you've fallen short, but also celebrating the fact that His grace is always enough. Let repentance be a time of renewal, where you invite God to cleanse your heart, restore your spirit, and set you on the path of righteousness. And most of all, let repentance be a time of hope, where you look ahead to the amazing future that God has planned for you.

In a world that often celebrates independence and self-reliance, repentance reminds us that we are not meant to do life on our own. We are completely dependent on God's grace, and that's something to rejoice in. God's grace is not a crutch; it's the foundation of our faith. It's what gives us strength when we are weak, hope when we feel lost, and peace in the midst of chaos. Repentance allows us to tap into that grace every single day, knowing that no matter how far we've strayed, God is always ready to welcome us back.

The road back to God is one that we will walk throughout our lives, but it's a road filled with beauty, transformation, and the love of a God who never gives up on us. As you continue on your journey, remember that repentance is not a burden, but a blessing. It's the road that leads us home, the path that restores our relationship with God, and the process through which we become more and more like Christ.

My prayer for you is that you will embrace this road with your whole heart, knowing that God's grace is more than enough to carry you through whatever challenges you face. As you walk the path of repentance, may you find the peace, joy, and freedom that come from being in the center of God's will. And may you always remember that the road back to God is never closed—it is always open, always welcoming, and always full of grace. Keep walking, keep trusting, and keep turning toward the One who loves you more than you can ever imagine. The journey of repentance is the journey back to the heart of God, and it's a journey worth taking every day of your life.

Don't miss out!

Visit the website below and you can sign up to receive emails whenever Joshua Rhoades publishes a new book. There's no charge and no obligation.

https://books2read.com/r/B-A-AJLBB-BYFCF

BOOKS 2 READ

Connecting independent readers to independent writers.

Did you love *Repentance Revealed The Road Back To God*? Then you should read *From Brokenness To Beauty Written By The Pen of Grace*[1] by Joshua Rhoades!

[2]

From Brokenness to Beauty: Written by the Pen of Grace is a profound journey into the heart of God's redemptive love. In a world where we often carry the weight of our brokenness—whether from personal mistakes, life's unexpected hardships, or the deep pain caused by others—this book serves as a beacon of hope. It reminds us that no matter how shattered we may feel, God's grace can transform our pain into something beautiful, rewriting the story of our lives with His endless love.

We all face moments when we feel lost, unsure of where to turn, burdened by regrets, and unsure of how to move forward. But God's grace is not just a comforting idea; it is the very force of His love, ever-present and powerful, working even in the messiest parts of our lives. Grace doesn't erase the past—it redeems it. Through every failure, every tear, every moment of despair, God's

---

1. https://books2read.com/u/47BJKN

2. https://books2read.com/u/47BJKN

grace is at work, taking what seems beyond repair and molding it into something greater than we could ever imagine.

This book invites you to see your brokenness through the eyes of grace, to trust that God is not finished with you yet, and to believe that no matter how incomplete or painful your story may seem, He is still writing it. In these pages, you'll discover that God uses the hardest chapters of our lives to showcase His love and healing. Let this be the start of your journey from brokenness to beauty, as you allow the loving hand of God's grace to rewrite your life into a testimony of His unending faithfulness.